The **Girls'** Book of

Wisdom

Edited by
Catherine Dee

D1451421

Little, Brown and Company
BOSTON   NEW YORK   LONDON

To my favorite girl in the world,
Jessie Langer. Hope she learns to read soon!

Compilation copyright © 1999 by Catherine Dee

First Edition

Cover photo in lower right by Jim Cummins/FPG International LLC; cover photos in upper right and lower left by Andrew Brilliant; black-and-white line illustrations throughout by Lou M. Pollack.
Thanks to Gwendolyn Brooks for permission to include an excerpt of her work: From *Blacks* (1991), by Gwendolyn Brooks. Copyright © 1991 by Gwendolyn Brooks. Reprinted with permission of Gwendolyn Brooks.

Library of Congress Cataloging-in-Publication Data

The girls' book of wisdom: empowering, inspirational quotes from over 400 fabulous females / edited by Catherine Dee. — 1st ed.
    p.   cm.
Includes index.
    Summary: A collection of quotations from over 400 famous women, including suffragists, pioneers, politicians, moms, musicians, athletes, and actors, grouped in such categories as "Friendship," "Confidence," and "Creativity."
    ISBN 0-316-17972-8
    1. Women Quotations Juvenile literature. [1. Women Quotations. 2. Quotations.]
    I. Dee, Catherine.
    PN6084.W6G57   1999
    305.4—dc21   99-24741

10 9 8 7 6 5 4 3 2 1

RRD-IN

Printed in the United States of America

Acknowledgments

First on this thank-you list are all the women and girls—past and present—who said all the wise and inspirational things in this book. Megan Tingley, my editor at Little, Brown, came up with the concept and provided great guidance. Jonathan Ganz, my sweetie; Sarah Dee, my sister; Fran Drake, my mom; and Orson Dee, my dad, provided feedback and cheerleading. Monica Johnson, Jane Press, Ed Ring, Peggy Benjamin, Jacqueline Kehoe, Kevin Weigler, and Warren Herr pored over the manuscript, offering wisdom about the wisdom. Jill Ehrhorn, Blinken Meynell, and Mary Godley searched the four corners of various libraries for girl-empowering material. Teacher Kathleen Clark asked her students to write their own quotes. Other assistance came from Scott Oberacker, Sheila Smallwood, and Hannah Mahoney at Little, Brown; Ed Chew, Anne Gulliver, Linda Levine, Jody Rohlena, Jacque Green, Jan Stoltman, Ruth Stevens, Jan Schmuckler, Craig Dale, Caterina Rando, Tony Rando, Clyde Lerner, Vivian Frederick, Terrilyn Chance, Jeff Voeller, Fran Harris, Ryan Dee, Vicky Langer, Alan Javurek, Hal Binder, Joan Larson, Pat Guy, and the editors and publishers affiliated with the quote sources.

Thanks to all!

Contents

Introduction

When women come together in one place to share their experiences, their dreams and wisdom, a very special resonance—a powerful energy—is created.
— **Marion Woodman,** psychologist

What if you could assemble hundreds of wise and accomplished women and girls who've lived in the past two centuries, and just listen to them share their pearls of wisdom? You would probably come away awed by their ideas, amazed by the similarities of some of their thoughts, and eager to try out their strategies yourself.

Well, here's your chance.

This book is filled with excellent advice and perceptive observations from more than four hundred exceptional women and girls. Every included quote was selected for its ability to inspire you. Some of these "pearls" are witty and entertaining, some are brilliant, and some are just plain helpful. Many are suggestions that women wish they'd been given when they were girls. These powerful quotes can change the way you see yourself and perceive the world.

The people quoted in this book are young and old, from the past and the present. They're scientists, musicians, business executives, activists, writers, athletes, actors, doctors, Internet pioneers, artists, moms, world leaders, daughters, and more. What they have to share can help you:

☆ Understand yourself

☆ Accept your body

☆ Feel confident

☆ Handle bad moods

☆ Overcome challenges

☆ Get motivated

☆ Break out of ruts

☆ Build good relationships

☆ Achieve great feats

☆ Have fun!

Of course, as a woman named Yula Moses once observed, "Wisdom is harder to DO than it is to know." It's easy to get all fired up, but putting ideas into practice takes effort.

However, knowing WHAT you can do, and being reminded that YOU CAN DO IT, is the fuel you need to get the fire started and keep it burning.

If you read this book from beginning to end, you'll see that it has a natural progression, but you can skip around, too. If you're looking for perspective on a certain issue, pick the chapter that most closely seems to match. Close your eyes and open the book to a random page when you want a little mood boost. Or read a few quotes every morning. Soon, the most meaningful ideas for you will become familiar and lodge themselves in your brain, where you can recall them anytime. Having "inherited" this valuable wisdom, you'll be better prepared to make any decisions, get through any situations, and live your life with conviction, enthusiasm, and joy.

Catherine Dee

I love [quotes] because it is a joy to find thoughts one might have, beautifully expressed with much authority by someone recognizedly wiser than oneself.

— **Marlene Dietrich,** actor, 1901–1992

Chapter I

Beginnings

*W*hen you wake up in the morning, do you make a mental note to enjoy the day?

When you're a kid, there's plenty of life *to* enjoy, because time seems to move in slow motion. But as you grow up, you'll feel like time is *speeding up*. Life is relatively short. That's why it's important to savor *right now*.

There are so many things to enjoy when you're young —your energy, your free time, your new experiences. So when you wake up each morning, remind yourself to appreciate every moment. Relish the basic activities, such as taking a hot shower, as well as the anticipated events, such as a friend's surprise party; and the unexpected delights, such as seeing a field of wildflowers. You've got a whole interesting day—and a whole fabulous life—ahead of you.

It's so quiet in the early morning darkness....Then the sun breaks....Fingers of light on the horizon....[I] just want to start singing or shout, "Glory Hallelujah!"
  —**Nora Dott Warren,** shrimper

I rise from sleep and say: Hail to the morning!
Come down to me, my beautiful unknown.
  —**Jessica Powers,** poet, nun, 1905–1988

Surely it's better to sleep late in the morning only when it's a rare privilege, not an everyday occurrence.
  —**Lauren Bacall,** actor

I have come to understand that every day is something to cherish.
  —**Kerri Strug,** gymnast

With the new day comes new strength and new thoughts.
  —**Eleanor Roosevelt,** First Lady, humanitarian, 1884–1962

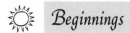

Each day I look for a kernel of excitement. In the morning, I say: "What is my exciting thing for today?" Then, I do the day.
—**Barbara Jordan,** lawyer, U.S. congresswoman, educator, 1936–1996

I wake expectant, hoping to see a new thing.
—**Annie Dillard,** writer

The preciousness of every moment is emphasized with every tick of the clock. Isn't it a magnificent day today?
—**Bel Kaufman,** writer, educator

Normal day, let me be aware of the treasure you are. Let me not pass you by in quest of some rare and perfect tomorrow.
—**Mary Jean Irion,** writer, teacher

Now, go take on the day.
—**Laura Schlessinger,** radio talk-show host

 # Self-Awareness

You know who the popular kids are at school, what they're thinking about and saying, and who and what impresses them . . . right?

The more important question: Do you know the same things about *you*? What are *you* thinking about and saying, and who and what impresses *you*?

You may not think much about self-awareness, but it is essential. If you don't know yourself, you could be swayed by what others think you should be, think, and do. That can interfere with your ability to make smart decisions and accomplish what *you* want in life.

So be a little self-centered! This doesn't mean being greedy or calling attention to yourself for no reason. It just means adding yourself to the list of people you want to impress.

Figuring out who you are is the whole point of the human experience.
>—**Anna Quindlen,** newspaper columnist, novelist

Without self-awareness we are as babes in the cradles.
>—**Virginia Woolf,** writer, 1882–1941

Nobody has a better vision of who you are than yourself.
>—**Sheryl Crow,** singer-songwriter

Deep inside us, there is a voice crying out.... It is a voice that can change our life.... It is the voice of our true self.
>—**Jinger Heath,** entrepreneur, business executive, writer

I think self-awareness is probably the most important thing towards being a champion.
>—**Billie Jean King,** tennis player

A child should be allowed to take as long as she needs for knowing everything about herself, which is the same as learning to be herself.
> —**Laura Riding,** writer, 1901–1991

Don't let others define you and tell you what you like or don't like, or what you can or can't do.
> —**Marsha Kinder,** professor, software developer, writer

It's where we go, and what we do when we get there, that tells us who we are.
> —**Joyce Carol Oates,** writer, editor

I am what I am.
> —**Alana Davis,** singer-songwriter

If I could know me, I could know the universe.
> —**Shirley MacLaine,** actor

Chapter 3

Journal Keeping

What if you were sick, but instead of giving you medicine, the doctor prescribed that you keep a journal?

It might sound funny, but it would be good advice. The simple act of reporting what's in your head and heart can make you feel better. Once upsetting thoughts and feelings have gone through your arm and down the pen to the paper, it feels natural to let them go. In addition, psychologists say that writing in a journal can build your confidence because it strengthens your self-awareness.

Get a blank notebook and start making journal entries. Don't worry about writing impressively, or about perfect spelling and grammar; this isn't a class assignment. You're the only one who should see your journal.

Save and read your old journals every now and then. You'll be amazed at how you've grown and changed.

Oh, so many things bubble up inside me....That's why in the end I always come back to my diary. That is where I start and finish.

　　—Anne Frank, diarist, 1929–1945

Writing is a tool of transformation and can shine the light on the inside, dispelling darkness, taking us through external layers, bringing us closer to our souls.

　　—Hillary Carlip, writer

Journal writing is a voyage to the interior.

　　—Christina Baldwin, writer

Writing is how I process existence; it's how I make meaning out of my life.

　　—Ellen McLaughlin, playwright

I rap out a sentence in my notebook and feel better.

　　—Florida Scott-Maxwell, writer, psychologist, 1883–1979

It makes me laugh to read over this diary. It's so full of contradictions, and one would think I was such an unhappy woman. Yet is there a happier woman than I?
— **Sophie Tolstoy,** diarist, 1844–1916

I write down what I want to accomplish for the day. But most of my writing is to remind me of why I am here and how much I like myself as a person...when I leave my room to face the world, I'm in a great mood.
— **Kristina Koznick,** slalom skier

Your journal is a place where your point of view on the universe matters.
— **Mary Pipher,** psychologist, writer

Keep a grateful journal. Every night, list five things that you are grateful for. What it will begin to do is change your perspective of your day and your life.
— **Oprah Winfrey,** TV talk-show host, actor, producer

13

It doesn't matter what you write in a journal. It matters that it is *yours*.
>—**Sark,** artist, writer

The most important thing you'll ever write is your journal, even if it's not the best thing you ever write.
>—**Jessica Wilber,** age fourteen, writer

My diary seems to keep me whole.
>—**Anaïs Nin,** writer, 1903–1977

Chapter 4

Solitude

*A*re you afraid of being seen alone because people might think you have no friends?

There's nothing wrong with the social benefits of hanging out with a group. But there's nothing wrong with being by yourself, either. Try spending a couple of hours alone (not watching TV), and see how you feel — you'll probably find it very relaxing to be just with yourself.

When you're alone, it's usually peaceful and quiet. For creative people, this is often when they're most productive. For anyone trying to solve a problem, it's when solutions are likely to present themselves.

For you, it could be just what's needed to balance out a crazy day.

What a lovely surprise to discover how unlonely being alone can be.
>   —**Ellen Burstyn,** actor

Solitude is the salt of personhood. It brings out the authentic flavor of every experience.
>   —**May Sarton,** writer, 1912–1995

Constant togetherness is fine—but only for Siamese twins.
>   —**Victoria Billings,** journalist

I restore myself when I'm alone. A career is born in public—talent in privacy.
>   —**Marilyn Monroe,** actor, 1926–1962

Inside myself is a place where I live all alone and that's where you renew your springs that never dry up.
>   —**Pearl S. Buck,** writer, 1892–1973

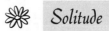

One lives and endures one's life with others … but it is only alone, truly alone that one bursts apart, springs forth.
　　—**Maria Isabel Barreno,** writer, poet

It's almost as if being alone is required if I'm to recognize myself.
　　—**Mary Chapin Carpenter,** singer-songwriter

Dining alone is definitely my thing. And going to the movies by myself is one of the most pleasurable things I do. I get my popcorn, licorice and a large soda, then I make a beeline for my favorite seat.
　　—**Tyra Banks,** model

I love to go somewhere where there's no sound except the wind and the trees.
　　—**Renee Zellweger,** actor

17

Being solitary is being alone well . . . luxuriously immersed in doings of your own choice, aware of the fullness of your own presence rather than of the absense of others.

—**Alice Koller,** writer

Writing to me is an addiction. I love the solitude.

—**Amy Tan,** writer

Got my mind in the clouds
And I want to feel cozy all alone

—**Randy Crawford,** singer

Only when one is connected to one's own core is one connected to others. . . . And for me, the core, the inner spring, can best be refound through solitude.

—**Anne Morrow Lindbergh,** writer

 Spirituality

On a warm night, go outside, lie down, and look up at the glittering night sky. Think about how many billions of stars are scattered in space, and how they got there.

This little exercise is sure to make you wonder how the earth came to exist and why you're here. That's where spiritual beliefs come in.

Why are spiritual beliefs important? Because they make you feel like you're not alone in the world, and that your life has higher meaning, and that's comforting.

What makes you feel spiritually connected? It could be praying, singing, dancing, or meditating. Or it could just be taking a walk in the forest or writing a poem. Whatever it is, make it a part of your daily routine.

It is this belief in a power larger than myself and other than myself which allows me to venture into the unknown and even the unknowable.

—**Maya Angelou,** poet, writer

The spiritual realm is the source of all the others.... There you are deepened and given the pattern as well as the purpose that guides your higher service in the world.

—**Jean Houston,** writer, philosopher, teacher

The process of life, from youth to middle age to old age to death, is to create something beautiful—the soul.

—**Ai Ja Lee,** acupuncturist, lecturer

It's very reassuring and spiritual to be connected with something larger than yourself and the inside of your own head.

—**Joan Osborne,** singer-songwriter

It is the bread of art and the water of my spiritual life that reminds me always to reach for what is highest within my capacities and in my demands of myself and others.

  —**Audre Lorde,** writer, educator, critic

We don't have to hunt for our spirituality. It's a by-product of living our lives.

  —**Anne Wilson Schaef,** writer, teacher, consultant

Discovering the spiritual center will lead to internal freedom and confidence.

  —**Adele Wilcox,** writer, minister

I may not be rich in material terms, but... I feel rich in spirit. That's all that counts to me.

  —**Amelia Rudolph,** dancer

Anything, everything, can be learned if you can just get yourself in a little patch of real ground, real nature, real woods, real anything ... and just sit still and watch.
   —**Lauren Hutton,** model, TV talk-show host

The externals are simply so many props; everything we need is within us.
   —**Etty Hillesum,** diarist, 1914–1943

We are not human beings trying to be spiritual. We are spiritual beings trying to be human.
   —**Jacquelyn Small,** writer

Invest in the human soul. Who knows, it might be a diamond in the rough.
   —**Mary McLeod Bethune,** educator, 1875–1955

✵ ✵ ✵

Chapter 6

Loving Yourself

"Women are good at shining kindness outward," observes artist and writer Sark, "yet if you ask how kind they are to themselves, they often cry." This is because they're sad that they don't treat themselves as compassionately as they do others, when there's no reason they shouldn't.

You deserve the same love, kindness, and undestanding that you offer to others. You are just as important as your friends. And your best friend should, of course, be you.

You must love and care for yourself, because that's when the best comes out.
> —**Tina Turner,** singer

Just as you would not neglect seeds that you planted with the hope that they will bear vegetables and fruits and flowers, so you must attend to and nourish the garden of your becoming.
> —**Jean Houston,** writer, philosopher, teacher

I've learned to take time for myself and to treat myself with a great deal of love and a great deal of respect 'cause I like me…. I think I'm kind of cool.
> —**Whoopi Goldberg,** actor

I feel beautiful whenever I think about my inner self.
> —**Nelly Hayatghaib,** age ten

When love begins with you, you no longer demand from others the love and sustenance you should give yourself.
—**Susan L. Taylor,** editor, writer

Remove those "I want you to like me" stickers from your forehead and, instead, place them where they truly will do the most good—on your mirror!
—**Susan Jeffers,** psychologist, speaker, writer

Make one's center of life inside of one's self, not selfishly or excludingly, but with a kind of unassailable serenity.
—**Edith Wharton,** writer, 1862–1937

I love myself when I am laughing. And then again when I am looking mean and impressive.
—**Zora Neale Hurston,** writer, 1891–1960

25

I have to be "in like with myself." When I'm not in like with myself, others won't be either!

—**Estella Hernandez Gillette,** program director

Chapter 7

Confidence

Which of these characteristics can't you be without when you're trying to achieve something?

- Popularity
- Niceness
- Confidence
- Looks

The answer is confidence. If you feel personally strong and powerful (the technical term for this is high self-esteem), you can do just about anything you want.

Don't worry if you don't feel especially confident at this moment. When you're a teen, you're still figuring out what's what. You're likely to grow more self-assured with time.

Confidence is something you can work to build throughout your life. Start now for best results!

Never bend your head. Always hold it high. Look the world straight in the eye.
—**Helen Keller,** writer, lecturer, 1880–1968

Women who are confident of their abilities are more likely to succeed than those who lack confidence, even though the latter may be much more competent and talented and industrious.
—**Joyce Brothers,** psychologist, writer

Who I am inside determines how I feel about my body instead of the other way around.
—**Alanis Morissette,** musician

Self-esteem isn't everything; it's just that there's nothing without it.
—**Gloria Steinem,** women's rights activist, writer

You have to know when to toot your own horn and how to do it properly.
>   —**Margaret King,** business executive

Don't compromise yourself. You are all you've got.
>   —**Janis Joplin,** singer, 1943–1970

When I walk into a room I assume I have to prove myself. I know that. I'm accustomed to that. But I also know I *can* prove myself.
>   —**Yvonne Brathwaite Burke,** former lawyer,
>   U.S. congresswoman

I am confident in myself because of what I do and who I am. I can do marvelous things!
>   —**Kaley Darga,** age twelve

I believe strongly in my own personal magic.
>   —**Susan Sarandon,** actor

Repeat an ego-boosting mantra to yourself: "I rule, I rule, I rule."

—**Sara Eckel,** writer

Beauty

$\mathcal{I}$t's time for some beauty news. No, not the kind about the hot new lipstick colors of the season, or how far your eyebrows should extend, or the wonders of diet shakes. This news flash is more newsworthy:

BEAUTY IS MORE THAN SKIN DEEP!

You're probably thinking that your mom or aunt has told you this a million times. It's not really news. But it's worth saying again: Real beauty has nothing to do with being a size five and having "pouty" lips. It is a reflection of your inner self—your personality and character.

Anybody worth knowing will like you for the person you are, not the sum of your measurements. And you have much more important things to think about, like doing well on the next math test, breaking a school track record, or running for student council.

Beauty is in the eye of the beholder, and it may be necessary from time to time to give a stupid or misinformed beholder a black eye.
　　—**Miss Piggy,** Muppet

The kind of beauty I want most is the hard-to-get kind that comes from within—strength, courage, dignity.
　　—**Ruby Dee,** actor, poet

Beauty to me is being comfortable in your own skin.
　　—**Gwyneth Paltrow,** actor

We must claim our bodies as our own to love and honor in their infinite shapes and sizes. Fat, thin, soft, hard, puckered, smooth, our bodies are our homes.
　　—**Abra Fortune Chernik,** writer

The self-confidence one builds from achieving difficult things and accomplishing goals is the most beautiful thing of all.
　　—**Madonna,** singer, actor

I believe that anyone who feels great with their body is in perfect shape.
>   —**Becky Cassler,** age ten

Can you imagine what would happen if girls took all the energy they spend worrying about their image and put it into painting, writing, theorizing, science, or sports?
>   —**Joan Jacobs Brumberg,** writer

I'm not going to let my life revolve around losing weight. I have other things to do.
>   —**Rosie O'Donnell,** TV talk-show host, comedian, actor

I define sexy as a real salt-of-the-earth woman who knows who she is, who feels strong and powerful.
>   —**Andie MacDowell,** actor

If you feel your value lies in being merely decorative, I fear that you someday might find yourself believing that's all that you really are. Time erodes all such beauty. But what it cannot diminish is the wonderful workings of your mind ...your humor, your kindness, and your moral courage.

> —**Susan Sarandon** as Marmee in the movie
> *Little Women*; Robin Swicord, screenwriter

I have known women who were not physically beautiful but who expressed themselves so magnificently that the result was an image of a beautiful woman.

> —**Marianne Williamson,** writer, speaker

If more of us would say, "This is my body — deal with it," the idea that there's a right size for breasts, or anything else, would evaporate.

> —**Donna Lou Bush,** writer

I like to think of people as flowers—there are many different colors, shapes, and sizes of flowers, and all of them are beautiful.
　　—Tech Girl, Web site animated character

The beauty that addresses itself to the eyes is only the spell of the moment; the eye of the body is not always that of the soul.
　　**—George Sand (Amandine-Aurore-Lucie Dupin,
　　baronne Dudevant),** writer, 1804–1876

Hey ho! There's more to life than cheekbones.
　　—Kate Winslet, actor

Chapter 9

Style

$\mathcal{W}$hat's your school's informal "dress code"?

Maybe it's long, baggy jeans and tank tops. A certain brand of shoes or wearing colorful clips in your hair.

Lots of girls dress in what's cool and wear their hair in the latest styles. But true style is more than just fashion and hair—it's personal flair. Your attitude and approach to life say as much about your style as your outfit. So even if you dress for comfort, you no doubt have your own unique style.

As a woman named Katharine Hamnett once said, "The best clothes are invisible…they make you notice the person."

What do you want people to notice about you?

Fashion can be bought. Style one must possess.
  —**Edna Woolman Chase,** fashion journalist, 1877–1957

I have lived in this body all my life and know it better than any fashion designer.... I am only willing to purchase the item which becomes me and to wear that which enhances my image of myself to myself.
  —**Maya Angelou,** poet, writer

The woman who dresses to suit her particular type, with only a moderate bowing acquaintance with fashion, comes out better than the woman who is a slave to the designer of the moment.
  —**Eleanor Roosevelt,** First Lady, humanitarian, 1884–1962

To me, anything that reflects that you have a positive outlook is fashionable.
  —**Serena Altschul,** TV reporter

Oh, never mind the fashion. When one has a style of one's own, it is always twenty times better.
—**Margaret Oliphant,** writer, 1828–1897

Being "well-dressed" is not a question of having expensive clothes or the "right" clothes—I don't care if you're wearing rags—but they must suit you.
—**Louise Nevelson,** sculptor, 1900–1988

If a woman discovers her own style she will automatically find creative outlets through which to express herself.... Personal style and self-confidence go hand in hand.
—**Alexandra Stoddard,** writer

What would happen if we dressed to feel good, to reflect our inner spirit, and forgot about projecting an image, looking thin, or wearing the right colors?
—**Jennifer Louden,** writer, workshop leader

Chapter 10

Health

We live in a largely "sit-down" world (e.g., watching TV, working at a computer), but our ancestors lived in a stand-up, extremely active one. This means our bodies genetically "remember" the benefits and pleasures of physical activity and expect us to provide them. If we don't, we aren't likely to feel so great.

You've heard the phrase "You are what you eat"? Obviously, if you eat greasy fries, you're not going to turn into one, but eating right will help you feel right.

Girls who exercise regularly enjoy improved concentration, clear thinking, and ease in falling asleep—not to mention muscle tone and strength. Exercise helps get rid of stress and depression. Plus, notes actor Jane Fonda, "Getting fit is a political act—you are taking charge of your life."

Health is not simply the absence of sickness.
— **Hannah Green,** writer

Get physical! Go to the woods and pick up a stick. Climb a mountain and look at the sky ... lift weights, go as far as your body tells you you can go.
— **Eartha Kitt,** dancer, actor, singer

Let fitness be your launching point. Picture exercise as the hub of a wheel with spokes that jut into every area of your life.
— **Judi Sheppard Missett,** aerobic dance pioneer

Bicycling has done more to emancipate woman than any one thing in the world.... It gives her a feeling of self-reliance and independence the moment she takes her seat; and away she goes, the picture of untrammelled womanhood.
— **Susan B. Anthony,** suffragist, 1820–1906

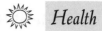

Exercise makes you more graceful. When you exercise you walk as if you own the street—with pride and fluidity.
　　—Sophia Loren, actor

It is central to girls to be physical. When girls stop playing outdoors, when they begin to refrain from the climbing and jumping and running, something changes.
　　—Andrea Johnston, writer, teacher

We are indeed much more than what we eat, but what we eat can nevertheless help us to be much more than what we are.
　　—Adelle Davis, nutritionist, 1904–1974

Food imaginatively and lovingly prepared, and eaten in good company, warms the being.
　　—Marjorie Kinnan Rawlings, writer, 1896–1953

43

I don't abuse my body, I don't put things in there that I shouldn't put in there.
> —**Jackie Joyner-Kersee,** track athlete

If you're going to get obsessive, be obsessed with your health, living long and having a career you love. When I'm doing that, I feel my best, no matter how much I weigh.
> —**Betty Carmellini,** member of the band Red Five

Food is an important part of a balanced diet.
> —**Fran Lebowitz,** writer, critic

It is never too early to start taking care of yourself.
> —**Jane Brody,** nutrition expert, writer, columnist

Health is a priceless gift from Spirit that most of us take for granted until we become sick.... If you have nothing else but your health, you are a wealthy woman.
> —**Sarah Ban Breathnach,** writer

God gave you only one body, so you better be nice to it.
   —**Sadie Delany,** educator, writer

☆ ☆ ☆

Chapter 11

Sports

What would you think if someone told you working out could be dangerous to your health? Only a few decades ago, doctors actually believed that even mild exercise could harm women's "fragile" bodies.

Now, of course, we know that just the opposite is true: Exercise *strengthens* our bodies. And we're in the middle of a female athletics revolution. Many women's sports, such as basketball, sailing, tennis, and swimming, are rivaling men's in popularity and prestige.

Fans get a lot out of watching women compete, but the athletes themselves get even greater benefits. Sports are not only a good way to get your exercise, they're a training ground for life, where you can practice teamwork, learn about competition, and experience the thrill of victory.

I use sports as a vehicle for learning: Just about everything you want to know is there.
　　　—Colleen Cannon, triathlete

The values learned on the playing field—how to set goals, endure, take criticism and risks, become team players, use our bodies, stay healthy and deal with stress—prepare us for life.
　　　—Donna de Varona, swimmer, TV sports commentator

With sports, you get the results back right away. With life, it's not always so black-and-white.
　　　—Rebecca Twig, cyclist

One of the most comon characteristics of my closest friends —each of whom are leaders in their respective fields—is that each was an athlete. Strengthening your body, working with others, and challenging yourself through sports will inspire and inform your life more than you could ever imagine.
　　　—Amelia Richards, women's rights activist, editor

I have learned discipline and how to listen to my body through sports.... I know what my limits are and how to perform at my best.

    —**Serena Altschul,** TV reporter

Skating, driving hoop and other boyish sports may be practised to great advantage by little girls.... It is true, such games are rather violent, and sometimes noisy, but they tend to form a vigorous constitution.

    —**Lydia Maria Child,** writer, abolitionist, suffragist, 1802–1880

The day I finally beat my brothers on the court was one of the sweetest victories I've ever experienced. They finally admitted, "It's got nothing to do with her being a girl. She's just good."

    —**Sheryl Swoopes Jackson,** basketball player

49

What do I do for fun? I sail. What do I do for work? I sail.
—**Dawn Riley,** sailor

Marathon swimming is the most difficult physical, intellectual, and emotional battleground I have encountered. And each time I win, each time I touch the other shore, I feel worthy of any other challenge life has to offer.
—**Diana Nyad,** swimmer

Sports can do so much. They've given me a framework: meeting new people, confidence, self-esteem, discipline, motivation. All these things I learned, whether I knew I was learning them or not, through sports.
—**Mia Hamm,** soccer player

Chapter 12

Creativity

*B*aking a pie? Building a fort in the backyard? Writing a computer program?

These are all creative acts. Creativity is simply the process of bringing something new into being. So if you've ever complained, "I'm not creative," it's time to create a new belief about yourself.

Creativity can make your life feel rich and rewarding. Cartoonist Lynda Barry is a big fan of letting your creative spirit come out to play. "Anything that gives you that strange inner delight you felt the first time you dumped silver glitter onto white glue lines that spelled out your name is worth doing," she explains.

So get out the glue, sequins, wax, wood, paper, wrench, guitar, flour, computer, or any other ingredients for your creative process, and start making stuff!

Helped are those who create anything at all, for they shall relive the thrill of their own conception, and realize a partnership in the creation of the Universe that keeps them responsible and cheerful.
—**Alice Walker,** writer, poet

Answering a creative need within affirms one's self-worth.
—**Mary Chapin Carpenter,** singer-songwriter

It's fun to be resourceful, to make a silk purse from a sow's ear.
—**Cynthia Rowley,** fashion designer

I just want to pick up my paintbrush and dip it into color, then stroke the paper to discover what comes forth.
—**Judy Chicago,** painter

Creativity comes with being human, it is the power to think new, to imagine, to see a metaphor. Animals make by instinct. People get new ideas. All you need is an open mind.
—**Jean Unsworth,** artist

Whether making art is your career or your hobby or your dream, it is not too late or too egotistical or too selfish or too silly to work on your creativity.

—**Julia Cameron,** artist, creativity expert, writer

Be adventurous. Try a lot of different things. Who cares if it doesn't work out? It's only paper!

—**Mary Engelbreit,** artist, business executive

One must also accept that one has "uncreative" moments.

—**Etty Hillesum,** diarist, 1914–1943

In writing, in art, personal expression is what people want. Women are taught to hide that, to fit the mold, to be chameleons. But people want to see who you are, what you're about.

—**Lynda Pearson,** advertising executive

It's really important that, as women, we tell our stories. That is what helps seed our imaginations.
  —**Ann Bancroft,** explorer

I believe that true identity is found in creative activity springing from within. It is found when one loses oneself.
  —**Anne Morrow Lindbergh,** writer

For me, creativity is self-generating. The energy that goes into my work comes back into my life.
  —**Rosanne Cash,** singer-songwriter

Ride into your life on a creative cycle full of juice, abundance and ecstatic wonderment.
  —**Sark,** artist, writer

Chapter 13

Dreaming

Imagine there's a crystal ball in front of you. Look in and see yourself sometime in the future.

What's going on? Where are you?

You've identified some of your deepest hopes and desires— your dreams.

Maybe they seem unlikely to come true anytime soon. That's OK. They *should* be a little out of reach. Dreams are supposed to push your limits.

The key thing about dreams is that you need to stay focused on them. They may seem distant and fuzzy now, but if you actively work toward them, you stand an excellent chance of making them real.

We should see dreaming as one of our responsibilities, rather than an alternative to one.
　　—**Mary Engelbreit,** artist, business executive

All acts performed in the world begin in the imagination.
　　—**Barbara Grizzuti Harrison,** writer, publicist

It's important to follow your wishing heart.
　　—**Lisa Loeb,** singer-songwriter

The future belongs to those who believe in the beauty of their dreams.
　　—**Eleanor Roosevelt,** First Lady, humanitarian,
　　1884–1962

Dreams come a size too big so that we can grow into them.
　　—**Josie Bisset,** actor

It is the soul's duty to be loyal to its own desires. It must abandon itself to its master passion.
—**Rebecca West,** writer, 1892–1983

When you think of it rationally, I don't even have the slightest hold on my dream; it's still all just fantasy. And yet, it's a potential reality.
—**Hannah Gosnell,** rower

Dream big dreams. If you are considering writing an article, develop it into a book. If you are writing a book, think ahead to your next project. Fill your days with ambitious goals.
—**Alexandra Stoddard,** writer

I can take a toothpick and make a lumberyard out of it.
—**Gladys Milton,** midwife

I dream, therefore I become.
—**Cheryl Grossman,** librarian, massage therapist

57

Dream up something you'd like to accomplish someday.
Then go out and accomplish it now!
   —**Debbie Tsai,** age fifteen

No one has ever achieved anything from the smallest to the
greatest unless the dream was dreamed first.
   —**Laura Ingalls Wilder,** writer, 1867–1957

 Intuition

Have you ever just "had a feeling" that you should do something? Have you ever had a problem and "known" the answer?

That's your intuition — your "sixth sense," or inner knowing. It may present a totally different perspective from the one your mind gives you, which can tell you only what makes sense logically and rationally. When you quiet your thoughts for a minute and invite your intuition to observe, you see a bigger picture. Your intuition can help keep you out of harm's way, assist you in doing what's right, and guide you to opportunities that have never even occurred to you.

Some people think women are more intuitive, which is why we have the expression "women's intuition." Do you have girls' intuition?

Intuition is when we know but we don't know *how* we know— it's knowing from the inside out.
—**Nancy Rosanoff,** writer

But still, the other voice, the intuitive, returns, like grass forcing its way through concrete.
—**Susan Griffin,** writer, educator

Intuition is a spiritual faculty and does not explain, but simply points the way.
—**Florence Scovel Shinn,** illustrator, philosopher, 1877–1940

Heed the still, small voice that so seldom leads us wrong, and never into folly.
—**Madame du Deffand,** intellectual, 1697–1780

Trust your hunches.... [They] are usually based on facts filed away just below the conscious level.
   —**Joyce Brothers,** psychologist, writer

I would say the best advice I've ever gotten is the best advice I ever give, and that's to listen to your heart more than anything else. Sometimes it's more about a feeling than thinking things through.
   —**Bobbi Brown,** entrepreneur, business executive

I have always been governed by my gut.
   —**Anna Quindlen,** newspaper columnist, novelist

Follow your instincts.... But you need to have all the information. To go on your instincts without being fully informed is, to me, the definition of folly.
   —**Deborah Norville,** TV show host

61

Don't always follow the crowd, especially if they are going the wrong way.

—**Lenore Jackson,** Internet specialist

Chapter 15

Risk

Girls often play it safe when they could accomplish much more by being a little gutsy. Some risks, such as walking down a dark alley at night or riding a bicycle without a helmet, are just plain dangerous. But others, such as tasting new foods or traveling to exotic places, are definitely worth taking.

Practice taking small risks, such as inviting the new kids in homeroom to lunch. Pretty soon you'll feel more comfortable taking bigger risks, such as trying out for the school play or doing a wilderness survival course.

If you take a risk and it doesn't pay off, don't think of it as a defeat. The reason risks are risky is that you're not *guaranteed* to benefit. Remember: *Taking the risk* is what counts, and you're sure to learn something valuable from every risk you take.

Risk!...Do the hardest thing on earth for you.
    —**Katherine Mansfield,** writer, 1888–1923

The day came when the risk it took to remain tight in a bud became more painful than the risk it took to blossom.
    —**Anaïs Nin,** writer, 1903–1977

A ship in port is safe, but that's not what ships are built for.
    —**Grace Murray Hopper,** mathematician, computer technology inventor, 1906–1992

I'll always push the envelope. To me, the ultimate sin in life is to be boring. I don't play it safe.
    —**Cybill Shepherd,** actor

Jump into the middle of things, get your hands dirty, fall flat on your face and then reach for the stars.
    —**Joan L. Curcio,** educator

If you risk nothing, then you risk everything.
    —Geena Davis, actor

If people aren't laughing at you, you aren't saying anything very unusual. So let your voice be loud and strong, dare to try things that may fail.
    —Joline Godfrey, girls organization founder, business executive, writer

Only she who attempts the absurd can achieve the impossible.
    —Robin Morgan, writer

Every time I catch myself saying, "Oh no, you shouldn't try that," I think, "Yes, I *should*."
    —Erica Jong, writer

If you're never scared or embarrassed or hurt, it means you never take any chances.
    —Julia Sorel, writer

65

There's risk all around, so security really has to be within yourself.... What you need to do is not hold yourself back.
—**Terry Patterson,** business executive

If I claim one guiding principle for my life, it is to say yes to unusual propositions and see what happens.
—**Barbara Brown Taylor,** minister

The only real risk is the risk of thinking too small.
—**Frances Moore Lappé,** nutritionist, ecologist

Loosen your girdle and let 'er fly!
—**Babe Didrikson Zaharias,** athlete, 1911–1956

 **Adventure**

What's your daily routine? Get out of bed, get ready for school, go to school, go to soccer or theater practice, come home, talk to your best friend on the phone, do your homework, eat dinner, curl up in bed?

Most people prefer having a fairly predictable life. But having routines can make us forget that life is supposed to be a wonder-filled journey.

So, how do you bring adventure to your daily grind? By looking for opportunities, however small, to *vary* your routine. For instance, walk home from school a different way. Read a book instead of watching your regular TV show. This week, go to a museum, sing karaoke, or enter the local newspaper's photography contest.

Pretty soon, adventures will be part of your routine, and your routine will no longer be, well…routine.

Life is either a daring adventure or nothing. To keep our faces toward change and behave like free spirits in the presence of fate is strength undefeatable.

—**Helen Keller,** writer, lecturer, 1880–1968

I've stayed in the front yard all my life.
I want a peek at the back
Where it's rough and untended and hungry weed grows.

—**Gwendolyn Brooks,** poet, writer, educator

Life is like a bus: you can get on and go somewhere or you can just sit there and watch it pass you by.

—**Debbie Tsai,** age fifteen

Do not stop thinking of life as an adventure. You have no security unless you can live bravely, excitingly, imaginatively.

—**Eleanor Roosevelt,** First Lady, humanitarian, 1884–1962

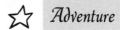

I'd like to get in a truck. That's what I'd like to do—get in a truck, and put in a cooler and a stove, and a little dresser drawer and a place for a cot…and take off across the country!
   —**Janet Reno,** U.S. attorney general

If you feel a little stiff, or bored, or dry…especially if you feel a lack of silly—slip some adventure into your life.
   —**Sark,** artist, writer

My favorite thing is to go where I've never been.
   —**Diane Arbus,** photographer, 1923–1971

Adventure can take many forms. Sometimes, following your heart is the greatest one of all.
   —**Dagny Scott,** editor

You can run out of unclimbed peaks. But if you're creative, you'll never run out of adventures.
   —**Nancy Feagin,** mountain guide

Chapter 17

Goals

Every year around December 31, people think about their New Year's resolutions. Some people make long lists, while others commit a few goals to memory.

But you don't have to wait until New Year's Eve to decide what you want to do with your life. Write down what's important to you and what you want to learn, achieve, or experience. Then think about the steps you'll need to take to accomplish these goals.

Setting a goal is like drawing a map to show where you want life to take you. With a goal in mind, you know where you're headed and you're less likely to get lost.

It's important to have a plan, a big picture. You can deviate from it or change it completely, but it gives you something to work for.

—**Shannon Miller,** gymnast

I believe the most important thing is not to lose the perspective of where one is heading.

—**Benazir Bhutto,** former prime minister of Pakistan

It's more important to know where you are going than to get there quickly. Do not mistake activity for achievement.

—**Mabel Newcomer,** writer

It has been said that goals are like magnets. They constantly pull us toward them.

—**Jinger Heath,** entrepreneur, business executive, writer

 *Goals*

I am always more interested in what I am about to do than in what I have already done.

> —**Rachel Carson,** environmentalist, marine biologist, writer, 1907–1964

Goals give us a reason to wake up and get out of bed every morning.

> —**Heather Hennessey,** age fifteen

If you help others obtain their goals and desires, you in turn will obtain your own.

> —**Teresa M. Moisant,** business executive

Sleep late…lounge in your jammies. Then get out of bed and plan how you're going to go after the next fabulous thing that you want.

> —**Kate White,** editor, writer

73

A good goal is like a strenuous exercise—it makes you stretch.

—**Mary Kay Ash,** entrepreneur, business executive

Chapter 18

Believing

When you were young, did you read *The Little Engine That Could*? It's about a train that gets stuck at the bottom of a hill. "I think I can...I think I can," chants the locomotive, and it goes chugging up the hill.

Of course, the moral of the story is: Believe in your abilities. If the train hadn't known it could make it, the book would have had a very unhappy ending.

Like the train, you have a little voice inside that's chanting the same thing: "I think I can, I think I can." Let it speak loudly, and trust it.

If there is faith that can move mountains, it is faith in your own power.
> —**Marie von Ebner-Eschenbach,** writer, 1830–1916

Never say you can't do it. Say you can or you will, and then do it.
> —**Jamiesa Turner,** age twelve

If you think you can, you can. And if you think you can't, you're right.
> —**Mary Kay Ash,** entrepreneur, business executive

The body achieves what the mind believes.
> —**Amy Fuller,** sailor, rower

When people keep telling you that you can't do a thing, you kind of like to try it.
> —**Margaret Chase Smith,** congresswoman, 1897–1995

It looks impossible until you do it, and then you find it is possible.
—**Evelyn Underhill,** mystic, 1875–1941

To succeed you have to believe in something with such a passion that it becomes a reality.
—**Anita Roddick,** entrepreneur, business executive

If you believe in yourself, if you believe in your dreams, and if you do your best at what you can do, you're going to be all right.
—**Carol Moseley-Braun,** former U.S. senator

It's all up to us. Remember, there were people who said the airplane couldn't fly.
—**Grace Murray Hopper,** mathematician, computer technology inventor, 1906–1992

☆ ☆ ☆

 # Action

You've got an exciting project planned. Maybe it's training to run a local race or painting a piece of furniture or starting your own Web zine. There's only one problem: You can't seem to get started!

That's procrastination, which is common among people of all ages. But sooner or later, if you want to achieve something, you've got to *get moving*.

Even highly successful women struggle with taking action. According to business executive Evelyn Lauder: "The hardest part of any project is beginning it." Once you get the ball rolling, though, you've got momentum, and whatever you're doing becomes easier.

Life has taught me one supreme lesson. That is that we must—if we are really to *live* at all...we must put our convictions into action.
> —**Margaret Sanger,** activist, 1879 –1966

It had long since come to my attention that people of accomplishment rarely sat back and let things happen to them. They went out and happened to things.
> —**Elinor Goulding Smith,** writer

The biggest sin is sitting on your ass.
> —**Florynce Kennedy,** lawyer

One of my rules is: Never *try* to do anything. *Just do it.*
> —**Ani DiFranco,** singer-songwriter

If you rest, you rust.
> —**Helen Hayes,** actor, 1900 –1993

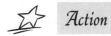

Action is the antidote to despair.
　　—Joan Baez, singer-songwriter

Do not wait for ideal circumstances, they will never come;
nor for the best opportunities.
　　—Janet Erskine Stuart, poet, writer, 1857–1914

Just put on your makeup and get out there and do it.
　　—Emma Bunton ("Baby Spice"), singer

Opportunity is like a hair on a bald-headed man; it only
comes around once and you have to grab it while it's there.
　　—Joycelyn Elders, former U.S. surgeon general

I don't believe in luck. We make our own good fortune.
　　—Joyce Brothers, psychologist, writer

Don't even make a list. Do everything right now.
　　—Sigourney Weaver, actor

So whatever you want to do, just do it. Do not worry about making a fool of yourself. Making a damn fool of yourself is absolutely essential. And you will have a great time.

—**Gloria Steinem,** women's rights activist, writer

Chapter 20

Thinking

Think of a time you analyzed a problem and came up with a solution.

Your brain processed a whole bunch of data and pieced it together like a puzzle. Pretty amazing.

Our power to reason and process information is a gift. Do you value and use this critical ability to its fullest potential? The adage "Use it or lose it" applies here, so put your brainpower to work. Don't let other people make decisions for you based on their own thinking. Try to think of the answers to jokes before you hear the punchlines. Develop your vocabulary. Take challenging courses. Invent things.

Your mind is full of great ideas. If you don't think of them, who will?

A usable mind is a most exciting possession.
 —**Mildred McAfee Horton,** college president

People like Einstein shouldn't be uncommon. All our minds have that potential. It's a matter of cultivating it, of taking responsibility for it.
 —**Jewel,** singer-songwriter

The most important part of the body is the brain.
 —**Frida Kahlo,** artist, 1907–1954

To think and to be fully alive are the same.
 —**Hannah Arendt,** sociologist, historian, 1906–1975

Your mind is like any other muscle—if you don't use it, it shrinks.
 —**Molly Ivins,** newspaper columnist

My brain doesn't have an idle.
 —**Linda Wachner,** company president

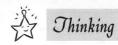

Thinking

To achieve, you need thought...that's real power.
   —Ayn Rand, writer, critic, 1905–1982

Our lives seem to be governed mostly by the advice of experts. [But] the more we think for ourselves, the less we shall need advice.
   —Laura Ingalls Wilder, writer, 1867–1957

To repeat what others have said, requires education; to challenge it, requires brains.
   —Mary Pettibone Poole, writer

If people see me as competent first, that's more of a compliment than saying, "She's really cute."
   —Sandra Bullock, actor

There's nothing so dangerous for manipulators as people who think for themselves.
   —Meg Greenfield, writer

85

To have ideas is to gather flowers; to think, is to weave them into garlands.

—Anne-Sophie Swetchine, writer, 1782–1857

Chapter 21

Speaking Out

"What have you got to say for yourself, young lady?"

If an adult has ever asked you that, you probably took for granted that you could present your side of the story. But women haven't always spoken their minds, and their opinions haven't always been valued. Some women have even been punished for expressing their views.

In the late 1800s, women's rights leader Elizabeth Cady Stanton broke the silence and issued a call to verbal action: "Every truth we see is ours to give the world, not to keep for ourselves alone, for in so doing we cheat humanity out of their rights and check our own development."

Point being? You have important things to say. So… what *have* you got to say for yourself?

Women have been trained to speak softly and carry a lipstick. Those days are over.

> —**Bella Abzug,** lawyer, politician, women's rights activist, 1920–1998

If you don't say it, nobody's going to know about it.

> —**Aliza Sherman,** entrepreneur, Internet expert, writer

I'm just saying what I think and if what I think happens to have some mature clarity, cool.

> —**Fiona Apple,** singer-songwriter

Each time a woman or girl speaks clearly and directly rather than deferentially, the status quo is budging into a new format.

> —**Montana Katz,** writer, speaker

Let us not forget that among [women's] rights are the right to speak freely.

> —**Hillary Rodham Clinton,** First Lady

People respect you when you say, "This is what I think and this is why I think it."
—**Lucy Berroteram,** business executive

I believe I'm here to speak my truth and that's all I have to do. I don't have to make people understand it; I don't have to make them agree. I just have to speak the truth.
—**Anne Wilson Schaef,** writer, teacher, consultant

I speak without reservation from what I know and who I am.
—**Ani DiFranco,** singer-songwriter

If I feel strongly, I say it. I know I can do more good by being vocal than by staying quiet.
—**Martina Navratilova,** tennis player

For me, words are a form of action, capable of influencing change. Their articulation represents a complete, lived experience.
—**Ingrid Bengis,** writer

The silence won't protect us. We gotta join together and speak out.
  —**Cybill Shepherd,** actor

As we become a nation of fewer widgets and more Web sites, a new premium has been put on the oldest form of communication: the ability to stand and say what you think in front of others.
  —**Peggy Noonan,** speechwriter

If you don't ask the question because it's "dumb," somebody else (probably a man!) will ask it, and people will say, "Oh, good question." No question is dumb, as one of my professors used to say.
  —**Sharon Craft Cooper,** aerospace engineer

I would say, express your feelings at all times. Unless you're trying to hide something.
  —**Miss Piggy,** Muppet

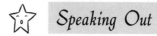

Courage consists of: the knowledge that you'll regret it... if you don't say what's on your mind.
   —**Grace Paley,** writer, teacher, activist

The appetite to be a spokesperson for your gender, for your race, for the whole species—to have this appetite is fabulous!
   —**Maya Angelou,** poet, writer

 # Learning

When are you "learning"?

At school, of course. But learning doesn't just happen in class. You learn new skills all the time, such as how to fix a broken lamp or cook a Thanksgiving turkey. You're constantly collecting new information on what you like, and how people behave. In discussions with friends, you may discover opinions you didn't know you had. You're constantly broadening your knowledge in every area of life.

Learning is like wearing a pair of 3-D glasses—it gives dimension to your existence. The more you know, the more colorful your world can be. So, put on your specs and start looking around!

The Girls' Book of Wisdom

I always keep myself in a position of being a student.
—**Jackie Joyner-Kersee,** track athlete

Nothing you learn, however wide of the mark it may appear at the time, however trivial, is ever wasted.
—**Eleanor Roosevelt,** First Lady, humanitarian, 1884–1962

Education is the jewel casting brilliance into the future.
—**Mari Evans,** writer

Literacy means liberation.
—**Septima Clark,** educator, civil rights activist, 1898–1987

A BMW can't take you as far as a diploma.
—**Joyce A. Myers,** business executive

Test scores do not determine what you will be when you grow up. Rather hard work and material learned do.
—**Jennifer Kwong,** scientist

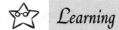

My philosophy is anyone or anything that gives you knowledge inspires you.

  —**Gabrielle Reece,** volleyball player

You never learn anything like you learn it by experiencing it.

  —**Alice Neel,** painter

Read all you can lay your hands on, from the label on the ketchup bottle to literature's masters. The rewards of reading never diminish and continue forever to broaden your horizons and bring pleasure to your life.

  —**Helen Ganz,** lawyer

I have learned the most from other people. Buy yourself a brain picker—ask a lot of questions.

  —**Tara VanDerveer,** basketball coach

The most beautiful thing in the world is, precisely, the conjunction of learning and inspiration. Oh, the passion for research and the joy of discovery!
   —**Wanda Landowska,** musician, 1879–1959

A good education is another name for happiness.
   —**Ann Plato,** poet, teacher, writer, 1820–?

 # Leadership

Do you have what it takes to be a leader?

Well, there's no designated personality type for leaders. All you need are a desire to make positive things happen, an ability to work hard, basic knowledge of how to motivate people, and "stick-to-it-iveness."

It's easy to find out if you have leadership potential—try organizing a project. Edith Weiner, a professional trend predictor, tells how: "The next time you are at work, at church, with your friends, or with your associates, suggest a challenge—you outline the work, you put the resources together."

Take charge today!

Toughness doesn't have to come in a pinstripe suit.
— **Dianne Feinstein,** U.S. senator

The only prerequisites to leadership are that you remain positive, calm, and open-minded.
— **Alexis Hunter,** age eighteen

You can lead by example. Feel competent within yourself.
— **Jenai Lane,** entrepreneur, business executive

Leadership is contagious. It moves from person to person; you can be the person who starts the epidemic.
— **Melva T. Johnson,** age eleven

The leadership instinct you were born with is the backbone. You develop the funny bone and the wishbone that go with it.
— **Elaine Agather,** bank president

I voted for my opponent because I thought it was polite. Well, he voted for himself, and I learned my lesson: If you believe in yourself, vote for yourself.

> —**Lynn Martin,** former U.S. secretary of labor, on running
> for class president against her boyfriend in eighth grade

We are coming down from our pedestal and up from the laundry room. We want an equal share in government and we mean to get it.

> —**Bella Abzug,** lawyer, politician, women's rights activist,
> 1920–1998

There is this idea that you can stay home and make the world better for your family—well, you can make it a whole lot better for a lot more people if you get out and do something about public policy.

> —**Pat Schroeder,** former U.S. congresswoman

The doors are open for us now, and we are streaming through them, as employees, executives, professionals, and entrepreneurs. Our brains and talent are taking us steadily to the top.

    —**Jane Bryant Quinn,** journalist

Women's place is in the House—and in the Senate.

    —**Gloria Schaffer,** political activist

Chapter 2 4

Power

It wasn't long ago that power was a male-only luxury.

Now those days are history. American women have economic power: They are starting more businesses than men and, in many professions, earning the same salaries. Women have political power: The large female segment of the population — 52 percent — has more voters, so it has the potential to change election results.

And you've probably heard about "girl power" — a slew of new books and programs focused on helping girls be strong and capable. Girls all over the country are realizing they can be the most influential generation in modern times.

You've got the power...now how are you going to use it?

Why, then, do women need power? *Because power is freedom.* Power allows us to accomplish what is important to us, in the manner that we best see fit.

— **Patti F. Mancini,** administrator

Power can be taken, but not given. The process of the taking is empowerment in itself.

— **Gloria Steinem,** women's rights activist, writer

Power...is not an end in itself, but is an instrument that must be used toward an end.

— **Jeane J. Kirkpatrick,** scholar, diplomat

Your passion is your true power. The more you discover and express your passion for life, the more irresistible you will become to others.

— **Barbara De Angelis,** writer, speaker

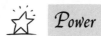

I do not wish [women] to have power over men; but over themselves.

> —**Mary Wollstonecraft,** writer, women's rights activist, 1759–1797

Power is the ability to take one's place in whatever course is essential to action and the right to have one's part matter.

> —**Carolyn G. Heilbrun,** writer

The first step toward liberation for any group is to use the power in hand....And the power in hand is the vote.

> —**Helen Gahagan Douglas,** U.S. congresswoman, actor, singer, 1900–1980

Power in the best sense is not power for yourself, but power that you share with your community.

> —**Ann Richards,** politician

 # Courage

Courage is defined by *Merriam-Webster's Collegiate Dictionary* as the "mental or moral strength to venture, persevere, and withstand danger, fear, or difficulty." In other words, *guts*.

You need courage to do lots of things, such as breaking up with a boyfriend who isn't respecting you, dealing with a serious illness, camping in the wilderness, or making up with your sister after a fight. If you're scared, it's OK—that's part of courage. "Feel the fear and do it anyway," advises a psychology slogan.

Being courageous is like being on a plane that takes off in a foggy rainstorm — it's kind of dark and scary. Then you rise through the clouds and into the brilliant, clear blue sky. You feel like you're on top of the world, and the fear has completely vanished.

Courage is the ladder on which all other virtues mount.
—**Clare Boothe Luce,** diplomat, writer, 1903–1987

Life shrinks or expands in proportion to one's courage.
—**Anaïs Nin,** writer, 1903–1977

The right way is not always the popular and easy way. Standing for right when it is unpopular is a true test of moral character.
—**Margaret Chase Smith,** congresswoman, 1897–1995

I would urge you to be as impudent as you dare. BE BOLD, BE BOLD, BE BOLD.
—**Susan Sontag,** writer

Courage is more exhilarating than fear and in the long run it is easier....Just a step at a time, meeting each thing that comes up, seeing it is not as dreadful as it appeared, discovering we have the strength to stare it down.
—**Eleanor Roosevelt,** First Lady, humanitarian, 1884–1962

You become courageous by doing courageous acts....
Courage is a habit.
—**Mary Daly,** writer

The uplift of a fearless heart will help us over barriers. No
one ever overcomes difficulties by going at them in a
hesitant, doubtful way.
—**Laura Ingalls Wilder,** writer, 1867–1957

It is better to be a lion for a day than a sheep all your life.
—**Elizabeth Kenny,** nurse, 1880–1952

Be courageous. It's one of the only places left uncrowded.
—**Anita Roddick,** entrepreneur, business executive

As you go along your own road in life, you will, if you aim
high enough, also meet resistance.... But no matter how tough
the opposition may seem, have courage still—and persevere.
—**Madeleine Albright,** U.S. secretary of state

107

Chapter 26

Adversity

Sometimes life's hard.

Let's say you had your heart set on making the cheer-leading team, but you were turned down. You're disappointed, but you decide not to let it get you down. You go out for basketball instead. You discover that you love the game, and you become a hoop-shooting star. This wins you a college scholarship to your first-choice school. When you look back on your life years later, you see that the initial "failure" was the best thing that ever could have happened to you.

The good news is that bummer times will eventually pass. And while you may be upset by them, you never know how they'll change and improve the course of your life.

When you get to the end of your rope—tie a knot in it and hang on.
> —**Eleanor Roosevelt,** First Lady, humanitarian, 1884–1962

You must never feel that you have failed. You can always come back to something later when you have more knowledge or better equipment and try again.
> —**Gertrude Elion,** biochemist

Character cannot be developed in ease and quiet. Only through experience of trial and suffering can the soul be strengthened, vision cleared, ambition inspired, and success achieved.
> —**Helen Keller,** writer, lecturer, 1880–1968

I believe in rainbows and all of that. But there are darker colors…and it's the shade that defines the light.
> —**Tori Amos,** singer-songwriter

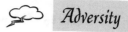

People think that when something goes "wrong," it's their fault. If only they had done something differently. But sometimes things go wrong to teach you what is right.
   —**Alice Walker,** writer

I've learned you can make a mistake and the world doesn't end.
   —**Lisa Kudrow,** actor

Oh, you must fail! If you don't fail, you don't know the degrees of success.... You have to fall down to learn how to [improve].
   —**Carol Bartz,** business executive

There is no such thing as failing. Failing is when you give up. Just move on and try something else.
   —**Tara VanDerveer,** basketball coach

111

Life does not accommodate you, it shatters you. It is meant to, and it couldn't do it better: Every seed destroys its container or else there would be no fruition.
    —**Florida Scott-Maxwell,** writer, psychologist,
        1883–1979

I believe everything happens for a reason and situations, even bad ones, make you stronger.
    —**Mya Harrison,** singer, age eighteen

I have a great belief in the fact that whenever there is chaos, it creates wonderful thinking. I consider chaos a gift.
    —**Septima Clark,** educator, civil rights activist,
        1898–1987

There are some things you learn best in calm, and some in storm.
    —**Willa Cather,** writer, 1873–1947

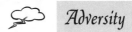

Don't get hung up on a snag in the stream, my dear. Snags alone are not so dangerous—it's the debris that clings to them that makes the trouble. Pull yourself loose and go on.
　　—Anne Shannon Monroe, writer, lecturer, 1877–1942

Remember, all dents are repairable!
　　—Jinger Heath, entrepreneur, business executive, writer

A clay pot sitting in the sun will always be a clay pot. It has to go through the white heat of the furnace to become porcelain.
　　—Mildred Witte Struven, mother of writer Jean Harris

113

Chapter 27

Perseverance

What do you do if you've been struggling to achieve something, but it hasn't happened yet?

You persevere: Hang in there and keep plugging.

Persistence is an art that not everyone can master. Why? Our society emphasizes things happening *fast*. For example, on TV shows, major problems are often resolved in half an hour. And with millions of people using e-mail, life is moving more and more at "Internet speed." As a result, some people don't want to stay in tough situations for the long haul; they'd rather have instant gratification.

Learning to be persistent may take time (of course). But once you have it, you'll be like the tortoise in "The Tortoise and the Hare," lumbering to the finish line.

Persistence is the twin sister of excellence. One is a matter of quality; the other, a matter of time.

—**Marabel Morgan,** writer

If I see a door comin' my way, I'm knockin' it down. And if I can't knock down the door, I'm sliding through the window.

—**Rosie Perez,** actor

Do not assume a door is closed; push on it. Do not assume if it was closed yesterday that it is closed today.

—**Marian Wright Edelman,** children's advocate, writer

If someone asked you, "Can you swim a mile?" you'd say, "Nah." But if you found yourself dumped out at sea, you'd swim the mile. You'd make it.

—**Gertrude Boyle,** business executive

It's 5% talent, 15% skill, and 80% hanging in there.
> —**Lucy Lawless,** actor

If you want to touch the other shore badly enough, barring an impossible situation, you will.
> —**Diana Nyad,** swimmer

When I look at the kids training today ... I can tell which ones are going to do well. It's not necessarily the ones who have the most natural talent or who fall the least. Sometimes it's the kids who fall the *most,* and keep pulling themselves up and trying again.
> —**Michelle Kwan,** figure skater

I don't try to work every day. I *do* work every day.
> —**Beatrice Wood,** artist

117

It doesn't take a genius to start a business. It takes someone relentless enough to go at it again and again and again.
— **Malia Mills,** swimwear designer, entrepreneur

Any road is bound to arrive somewhere if you follow it far enough.
— **Patricia Wentworth,** writer, 1878–1961

When people say, "It can't be done, or you don't have what it takes," it makes the task all the more interesting.
— **Lynn Hill,** rock climber

Diamonds are only chunks of coal,
That stuck to their jobs, you see.
— **Minnie Richard Smith,** poet

Never let well enough alone.
— **Joyce Brothers,** psychologist, writer

☆ ☆ ☆

 Optimism

Who's the most upbeat person you know? Chances are that she or he is well loved and fun to be around. And probably successful in life, too. Being optimistic is key in accomplishing almost anything, from finding a missing sock to getting your driver's license.

It's not natural to be cheery all the time, but try replacing pessimism with optimism whenever you can. For example, tackle a challenging homework assignment thinking to yourself, *I can ace this!* instead of *I could really blow it here!*

"Think positive" may sound dumb, but it's a tried and true strategy. If you expect the best, you just might get it.

We may not be able to change an outer circumstance, but we do have a choice in how we perceive it and react to it. A positive attitude is a powerful thing.
> —**Hillary Carlip,** aurthor

Attitude will take you further than talent.
> —**Ruthie Bolton-Holifield,** basketball player

I make the most of all that comes and the least of all that goes.
> —**Sara Teasdale,** poet, 1884–1933

You should promote the most positive, but the most genuine spin on things…people will just dig your energy.
> —**Lucy Lawless,** actor

I try to extract something positive from [every] situation, even if it's just learning not to make the same mistake twice.
> —**Claudia Schiffer,** model

You don't get to choose how you're going to die. Or when.
You can only decide how you're going to live. Now.
 —Joan Baez, singer-songwriter

All you need is positivity.
 —The Spice Girls, singers

Could we change our attitude, we should not only see life
differently, but life itself would *be* different.
 —Katherine Mansfield, writer, 1888–1923

From every scrap you make a blanket.
 —Rose Chernin, writer

Chapter 29

Humor

Have you ever noticed how great it feels to laugh at a funny joke or at your own silly antics?

The power of laughter lies in its ability to improve your state of mind. When you laugh, your body actually has a physiological reaction: Your brain releases anti-depressant biochemicals. This means that if you've been feeling down, you could feel better right away.

If you're a funny person, don't be afraid to let it show. Everybody likes being around someone who can make them smile.

Life is full of unexpected goofy and hilarious moments. Don't let them go by without giving them the laughs that they—and you—deserve!

Laughter is by definition healthy.
— **Doris Lessing,** writer

You have to have a sense of humor about your work and everything else in life. More and more, life and humor are inseparable for me.
— **Ani DiFranco,** singer-songwriter

There is nothing like a gleam of humor to reassure you that a fellow human being is ticking inside a strange face.
— **Eva Hoffman,** writer

There's something refreshing about a beautiful woman who's not afraid to make a fool of herself.
— **Sheryl Altman,** interviewer, writer, editor

[S]he who laughs, lasts.
— **Mary Pettibone Poole,** writer

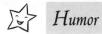

A good laugh overcomes more difficulties and dissipates more dark clouds than any other one thing.
>—**Laura Ingalls Wilder,** writer, 1867–1957

Laughter can be more satisfying than honor; more precious than money; more heart cleansing than prayer.
>—**Harriet Rochlin,** writer

Laugh as much as possible, always laugh. It is the sweetest thing one can do for oneself and one's fellow human beings.
>—**Maya Angelou,** poet, writer

A good laugh makes any interview, or any conversation, so much better.
>—**Barbara Walters,** TV reporter, talk-show host

Laugh and the world laughs with you;
Weep, and you weep alone.
>—**Ella Wheeler Wilcox,** writer, 1850–1919

*I*f you're like most girls, you sometimes feel cranky, angry, depressed, or sad. You wish you felt cheerful, but you can't seem to shake the bad mood.

Take heart — being in a grumpy mood isn't fun, but it may not last very long. Moods, by definition, usually change. A bad mood is like being on a seesaw seat that has hit the dirt; the only place to go is up.

Next time you get bent out of shape emotionally, try to be patient. Allow yourself to experience the sad, irritated, or mad feelings, which will help you get past them. Remember: The seesaw is likely to lift off soon and you'll be heading toward more cheery times.

Sadness is more or less like a head cold—with patience, it passes.
—**Barbara Kingsolver,** writer

The more lost you are, the more you have to look forward to.
—**Calista Flockhart,** actor

In the world there is a balance of good and bad, so when a bad day comes, know that a good day is just around the corner.
—**Margaret Sullivan,** age seventeen

Being crabby is real and it's healing. It can help us get closer to what's wrong, or what hurts.
—**Sark,** artist, writer

The basic trouble with depression is that it is so depressing. ...It often helps to look on the bright side. Make a teensy list of things that have not happened that really would be depressing if they had.
—**Miss Piggy,** Muppet

Sometimes you hug your pillow and cry at night, but this doesn't mean that life is bad. It just means that's the way it is. Life is rich.
    —**Goldie Hawn,** actor

I still want to cry in the middle of the night every now and then, y'know. And I won't stop doing that just because things are going swimmingly.
    —**Kate Winslet,** actor

Think of crying as singing. You wouldn't want to keep a song inside when you had an urge to sing. Crying reminds us that we're moved by life's sorrows and beauties and we're participating in them all fully.
    —**Alexandra Stoddard,** writer

If we had no winter, the spring would not be so pleasant.
    —**Anne Bradstreet,** poet, 1612–1672

Chapter 31

Family

If you're in trouble, whom do you turn to for help? Odds are it's a family member—your mother, father, sister, brother, cousin, aunt, or uncle—who will support you in what you're going through.

You may be thinking, *Yeah, right—my brother is such a little brat!* or *My aunt forgot my birthday for the fourth year in a row!*

That's normal. Just because you love your family doesn't mean they don't sometimes get on your nerves. But they're still your family. They've known and loved you since you were a baby. And they make up a vital network that you can rely on for advice and guidance throughout your life.

The family is the building block for whatever solidarity there is in society.

>—**Jill Ruckelshaus,** government official, speaker

Call it a clan, call it a network, call it a tribe, call it a family. Whatever you call it, whoever you are, you need one.

>—**Jane Howard,** writer

Thankfully, I have my family around me—people who'll tell the truth. If my hair is messed up, they'll be like, "Yo, Lauryn, that looks funny."

>—**Lauryn Hill,** singer

Family faces are magic mirrors. Looking at people who belong to us, we see the past, present and future. We make discoveries about ourselves.

>—**Gail Lumet Buckley,** writer

132

Most of all the other beautiful things in life come by twos and threes, by dozens and hundreds. Plenty of roses, stars, sunsets, rainbows, brothers and sisters, aunts and cousins, comrades and friends—but only one mother in the whole world.
— **Kate Douglas Wiggin,** writer, educator, 1856–1923

I think I get my drive from [my father]. He seized what was offered and proved that it doesn't really matter where you come from, it's where you're going.
—**Aimee Mullins,** disabled track athlete

A mother's arms are more comforting than anyone else's.
—**Diana, Princess of Wales,** 1961–1997

My dad taught me how to take care of myself. When I was in school and the kids were picking on me…he said, "If they challenge you to an after-school fight, you tell them you won't wait—you can kick their butt right now."
—**Cameron Diaz,** actor

Whenever I see someone on her birthday, I make a point to ask her, "Have you called your mom today and said thank you?"
— **Jamie Lee Curtis,** actor

My dad…always talked about determination and the importance of a positive attitude. He can make anything sound good even if it's not.
— **Shannon Dunn,** snowboarder

When you're jumping so high for something so far up in the sky, you have to know that there is definitely someone there who can catch you, someone who knows how to catch you and when. Mom is just that way.
— **Picabo Street,** skier

My father instilled in me that if you don't see things happening the way you want them to, you get out there and make them happen.
— **Susan Powter,** health expert

A sister is like a permanent best friend.
>—**Jacqueline Kehoe,** age fourteen

There is no friend like a sister / In calm or stormy weather; / To cheer one on the tedious way, / To fetch one if one goes astray, / To lift one if one totters down, / To strengthen whilst one stands.
>—**Christina Rossetti,** poet, 1830–1894

My brothers have been my role models all through my life. They set the standard for me.
>—**Cammi Granato,** hockey player

Is solace anywhere
more comforting
than in arms of sisters?
>—**Alice Walker,** writer, poet

Chapter 32

 # Mom's Advice

Who's your most incredible role model?

If you answered "My mother," you're not alone. Girls often have special relationships with their moms, and it makes sense. Who else cares as much, and who else could have so many wise ideas and philosophies to share with you? After all, she was once where you are now—she went through adolescence and lived to tell about it.

Artist Mary Engelbreit remembers her mother telling her, "Don't worry—someday your ship will come in." Mary's ship did indeed come in—she grew up and became a world-famous illustrator.

What helpful wisdom has your mom given you?

My mother gave me a bumblebee pin when I started work. She said: "Aerodynamically, bees shouldn't be able to fly. But they do. Remember that."

   —**Jill E. Barad,** business executive

I remember telling my mother, "When I get older, I'm going to be a man." "No, honey," my mother said. "God made you a young lady; He wants you to be a woman when you get older."

   —**Janet Jackson,** singer

She told me to stand up for what I believe in and not let people walk over me.... She convinced me that I wasn't really fat and that even if I was, it didn't matter.

   —**Clementine Shepherd,** age seventeen, daughter of actor Cybill Shepherd

When I was a teenager I rejected almost anything my mother said with a "What does she know?" Now that I'm an adult, her words of advice have come to drive my every day: "Be safe. Be who you want to be. Do what you want to do."
>—**Amelia Richards,** women's rights activist, editor

My mother instilled in me, "Make your own money, get your own career together, and then if you happen to meet a great guy, you'll meet him on a good level."
>—**Sandra Bullock,** actor

My mama told me that as long as you're on this earth, if everybody likes you, then you're not doing something right.
>—**Merlene Davis,** newspaper columnist

My mom's main philosophy has always been to follow your spirit where it leads you. She made me feel beautiful, smart, and powerful, that I could do anything.
>—**Rosanne Raneri,** singer-songwriter

139

When my mother first suggested I submit some scribbles to a comic-strip syndicate, I pointed out that I knew nothing about comic-strip syndicates or comic strips...[and] I did not know how to draw, she said, so what? You will learn.
　　—**Cathy Guisewite,** cartoonist

By believing in me [my mother] helped me believe in myself. She told me nothing was impossible.
　　—**Lilly Melgar,** actor

[My mother] was very demanding in terms of her own work. "Do it well, do it thoroughly," she'd say, "whatever you do."
　　—**Ruth Simmons,** college president

[My mother] taught me to have a good time!
　　—**Meryl Streep,** actor

Friends

Who's your best friend? Why?

Best friends—and other friends—are treasures in the truest sense. They're the ones who see eye to eye with you, and with whom you feel totally comfortable. They're the ones who tell you when you deserve better, rush to your side in an emergency, make you giggle, and celebrate your victories.

It may be hard to imagine, but when you move out, begin a career, and/or get into a love relationship, you could lose touch with some of your old pals. Avoid this loss as you get older by making a special effort to get together on a regular basis. Then the connections you've developed will continue to grow and enrich your life.

A good friend is a connection to life—a tie to the past, a road to the future, the key to sanity in a totally insane world.

    —**Lois Wyse,** writer

I am thankful for my friends because they are there when the good times aren't.

    —**Maria Brown,** age fifteen

Women rely on friends. . . . That's where we draw sustenance and find safety. We can count on our women friends when we need a good laugh or a good cry.

    —**Cokie Roberts,** TV and radio journalist, writer

I think best friends are the ones who have been through what you've been through. They understand where you're coming from and where you're going.

    —**Shannon Miller,** gymnast

We're a band, but we started off as friends and we'll end up as friends.

> —**Melanie Chisholm** ("Sporty Spice"), singer

Women's propensity to share confidences is universal. We confirm our reality by sharing.

> —**Barbara Grizzuti Harrison,** writer, publicist

Girlfriends are those women who know us better than anyone (sometimes better than we know ourselves). They are not only essential for coping with our day-to-day frustrations or sharing private jokes, they... help us grow as women and human beings.

> —**Carmen Renee Berry,** body worker; **Tamara Traeder,**
> publisher, lawyer; writers

It's always more meaningful and wonderful when you can share your life and goals with others. Great friends and family are key.

> —**Missy Giove,** mountain biker

I think we are realizing that the relationships we have with our girlfriends are as important as the career, as important as the marriage. They are sovereign.

 —**Rebecca Wells,** writer

My means of empowerment has always been to search out wonderful friends, people who believe in me, who help me believe in myself.

 —**Sandy Warshaw,** activist

The only good teachers for you are those friends who love you, who think you are interesting or very important, or wonderfully funny.

 —**Brenda Ueland,** writer, educator, 1891–1985

Each friend represents a world in us, a world possibly not born until they arrive.

 —**Anaïs Nin,** writer, 1903–1977

 *Love & Romance*

$\mathcal{A}$sk any woman to tell you about her first crush. She's likely to get a dreamy look on her face—smiling and recounting the experience as if it were a delicious dessert. Maybe you can relate…or maybe you just have a fantasy of falling madly and passionately in love with the hottie in your math class.

Romantic moments are bliss, but it helps to know some "women's wisdom" if you want a lasting partnership. What are the secrets of making a relationship work? A big one is realizing that other people can't meet *all* your needs, even if they try hard. If you keep that in mind, and strive to meet those other needs yourself, you'll stand a good chance of finding lasting love.

We love because it is the only true adventure.
   —**Nikki Giovanni,** poet

A guy doesn't have to be Brad Pitt, he doesn't have to have some great car, and he doesn't have to be a rocket scientist. He just has to be there when you need him.
   —**Shania Twain,** singer-songwriter

A lot of [women] seem to think that they need a man in order to feel secure or to be accepted. I may decide I want a boyfriend someday, but I don't *need* one.
   —**Latrice Davis,** age seventeen

The ultimate [in a relationship] is finding a place where you have no inhibitions, nothing to hide, where you can learn with one another.
   —**Jennifer Aniston,** actor

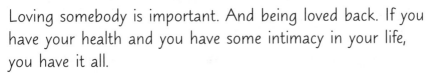

Loving somebody is important. And being loved back. If you have your health and you have some intimacy in your life, you have it all.

—**Sherry Lansing,** business executive

I now understand, at long last, that in a great relationship you can still maintain all the things that make you happy. I think a lot of my misunderstanding of relationships was in thinking I had to evaporate to be someone's girlfriend.

—**Julia Roberts,** actor

I could never be with someone who didn't have his own career, own life. I wouldn't want my boyfriend following me all over.

—**Steffi Graf,** tennis player

Whoever said love is blind is dead wrong. Love is the only thing that lets us see each other with the remotest accuracy.

—**Martha Beck,** writer

Woman should stand beside man as the comrade of his soul, not the servant of his body.
> —**Charlotte Perkins Gilman,** writer, lecturer, 1860–1935

My ideal man…has a great sense of humor. If I can't laugh with a guy, forget it.
> —**Kate Hudson,** actor

Partnership, not dependence, is the real romance in marriage.
> —**Muriel Fox,** public relations executive

One of the great riches I think about [our] marriage is [that] we were friends before we became more serious, and it's that friendship plus our relationship that is an enormous strength.
> —**Mary Robinson,** U.N. official, former president of Ireland

The truth is that love is the best feeling to have in this world.
> —**Lauren Bacall,** actor

[My husband] Tom still has to ask me out for a date.... I don't think you should just assume anything or take the other person for granted.

—**Nicole Kidman,** actor

I can negotiate my own deal, but it's nice to have the door opened for me or the wine poured. I love chivalry.

—**Tori Amos,** singer-songwriter

Nothing in life is as good as the marriage of true minds between man and woman. As good? It is life itself.

—**Pearl S. Buck,** writer, 1892–1973

 Self-Reliance

You've probably heard those songs playing on the radio. You know, the ones with lyrics like "Lean on me" and "How can I *live* without you?"

While these sentiments may seem affectionate, the message suggests that the singer can't make it on her or his own. It's great to have friends, family, and lovers to support you, but you don't want to be so dependent on them that you can't function without their help. You *can* live without someone; you *can* rely on yourself.

Being independent gives you the strength to get through hard times and get things done. As actor Katharine Hepburn put it, "As one goes through life one learns that if you don't paddle your own canoe, you don't move."

I am strong, I am invincible, I am woman.
—**Helen Reddy,** singer-songwriter

I have always had a dread of becoming a passenger in life.
—**Margrethe II,** queen of Denmark

I take care of myself, because I learned early on that I am the only person in life who's responsible for me.
—**Halle Berry,** actor

I ain't no damsel in distress
and I don't need to be rescued.
—**Ani DiFranco,** singer-songwriter

Never grow a wishbone, daughter, where a backbone ought to be.
—**Clementine Paddleford,** journalist, editor, 1900–1968

There is a richness in a life where you stand on your own feet.... You set your own ground rules, and if you follow them, there are great rewards.
> —**Margaret Bourke-White,** photographer, 1904–1971

Woman must not depend upon the protection of man, but must be taught to protect herself.
> —**Susan B. Anthony,** suffragist, 1820–1906

Independence I have long considered as the grand blessing of life, the basis of every virtue.
> —**Mary Wollstonecraft,** writer, 1759–1797

There is no such thing as being too independent.
> —**Victoria Billings,** journalist

If it is to be, it is up to me.
> —**Shirley Hutton,** business executive

Chapter 36

Money

In our society there's lots of emphasis on money and how to spend it. You know how nice it is to have cash—whether from an allowance or a summer job—so you can buy fun things like CDs or a pair of cool new boots. Later on, you'll need money to pay bills (e.g., rent) and save for your future.

You may be lucky, at times, to receive gifts of money or be supported by your parents or spouse; or you may get no assistance. Either way, it's important to earn *your own* money. "Bringing home the bacon" means you've got the resources to be independent, in control, and comfortable throughout your life.

A woman must have money and a room of her own.
—**Virginia Woolf,** writer, 1882–1941

If there is one universal lesson, it is that you should never be totally dependent on another individual for your income.
—**Ann Richards,** politician

You have to be financially responsible, or your independence gets taken away.
—**Jodie Foster,** actor, director, movie producer

[My daughter] says she wants to marry a rich man, so she can have a Porsche. My rejoinder always is: Go out and get rich yourself, so you can buy your own.
—**Carol Royce,** radio station administrator

Every woman should be able to turn her labor, either mental or manual, into money.
—**Virginia Penny,** writer, 1826–?

I just made up my mind that the only way I was going to have [money] is to work for it and earn it. That way no one can take it away from me.

    —**Margie Cunha Irvin,** coal miner

Women and girls have to *own* a part of the system—stocks, bonds, a business—if we aren't going to *be owned* by it.

    —**Joline Godfrey,** girls organization founder, business executive, writer

I think the girl who is able to earn her own living and pay her way should be as happy as anybody on earth.

    —**Susan B. Anthony,** suffragist, 1820–1906

Supporting myself at an early age was the best training for life I could possibly have received.

    —**Lea Thompson,** actor

Financial independence is one of the strongest things a woman can bring to a relationship.
—**Valerie Coleman Morris,** TV reporter

When you are in control of your money, you are in control of your life.
—**Elinor Lenz,** writer, educator

Chapter 37

Work

Do you know the secret of success?

It's not being brilliant. It's plainly and simply *hard work*.

As they say, you can't get something for nothing. You've got to practice your trumpet lessons if you want to be in the band, conjugate verbs if you want to become fluent in another language, and do aerobics (or some other form of exercise) to get buff.

When hard work pays off, it feels great to earn the rewards and know that you deserve them. Plus, believe it or not, work can be fun in and of itself.

So, what are you waiting for? Get to work!

I believe in hard work. It keeps the wrinkles out of the mind and the spirit.
> —**Helena Rubinstein,** business executive, philanthropist, 1882–1965

Do not feel entitled to anything you do not sweat or struggle for.
> —**Marian Wright Edelman,** children's advocate, writer

Winning isn't about miracles on ice, it's about training.
> —**Michelle Kwan,** figure skater

It would be magical to believe in fate, but I don't know if I do. I believe in working hard and being open to situations and opportunities.
> —**Lisa Loeb,** singer-songwriter

I do not know anyone who has got to the top without hard work. That is the recipe.
> —**Margaret Thatcher,** former prime minister of Britain

Some folks today want to do things the easy way. We have a saying, "They want to get there—without going!" And there isn't any such thing.... You've got to work for it.
— **Bessie Delany,** dentist, writer

The idea of a workout is to work harder than you ever would have to in a game. That way the game seems easy.
— **Krista Gingrich,** high-school basketball player

This is the day of instant genius. Everybody starts at the top, and then has the problem of staying there. Lasting accomplishment, however, is still achieved through a long, slow climb and self-discipline.
— **Helen Hayes,** actor, 1900–1993

I don't know anything about luck.... Luck to me is something else: hard work.
— **Lucille Ball,** comedian, actor, 1911–1989

161

When I was fifteen, I had lucky underwear. When that failed, I had a lucky hairdo, then a lucky race number, even lucky race days. After fifteen years, I've found the secret to success is simple. It's hard work.
— **Margaret Groos,** marathon runner

Every day you push, you grow, you drive yourself to go beyond where you are. I think if you do it right, you never stop growing — but just like building muscles, it gets easier after a while.
— **Catherine Collins,** NASA official

Laziness may appear attractive, but work gives satisfaction.
— **Anne Frank,** diarist, 1929–1945

Career

Working women have tons of good career-planning advice for girls. But more than anything else, they'll tell you: Plan to do work that you *love!*

This is critical because your career is likely to be a big part of your life. You'll want to be doing something that you enjoy and find challenging, with people you like.

You don't need to decide your career options right now. However, your interests could hold clues to the possibilities. The skills you develop in hobbies could be ones you end up using in a job. If you explore new interests and learn about what you like to do now, you'll be well prepared when you start considering careers.

Do what you love; the money will follow.
　—**Marsha Sinetar,** writer

If you always do what interests you, then at least one person is pleased.
　—**Katharine Hepburn,** actor

Whether we call it a job or a career, work is more than just something we do. It is a part of who we are.
　—**Anita Hill,** law professor

People think at the end of the day that a man is the only answer [to fulfillment]. Actually a job is better for me.
　—**Diana, Princess of Wales,** 1961–1997

I enjoy working like other people enjoy taking vacations.
　—**Nanci Mackenzie,** entrepreneur, business executive

The mix of our ambitions and our cleverness—the ability to piece together work that will both satisfy and support us—is the secret to surviving, even thriving.
—**Wendy Reid Crisp,** business executive, writer

The career is…my life…I feel *home.*
—**Neepa Ved,** medical student

I thought there would be just one door, with one career choice behind it. I've been amazed to find that there are so many doors with so many choices, so many surprises.
—**Marcia Vaughan,** children's book author

There might be false starts and do-overs. You are entitled to experiment before you find your calling.
—**Jane Pauley,** TV journalist

A career is like hair color: There's no harm in considering a change.
—**Téa Leoni,** actor

Choose to have a career early and a family late. Or choose to have a family early and a career late—but plan a long life.
   —**Janet Rowley,** doctor

If you find something you really love as you're growing up, look hard to see if you can make a living at it instead of giving it up for something more sensible.
   —**Jennifer Lamb,** stuntwoman

For true independence you have to make a job, not just take a job.
   —**Joline Godfrey,** girls organization founder, business
      executive, writer

Whatever the job you are asked to do at whatever level, do a good job because your reputation is your resume.
   —**Madeleine Albright,** U.S. secretary of state

Chapter 39

Success

Think of something you've done that makes you proud. Maybe you danced in a school play that got rave reviews, won a 4-H competition, organized a beach cleanup, or pulled off some other noteworthy feat.

Congratulations! Achievements like these are a big deal, and they don't happen every day.

You probably accomplished what you're proud of by using skills discussed in this book, such as believing in your abilities, thinking optimistically, and working hard. It's also likely that you progressed through "milestones" on your way to the goal. As entrepreneur Mary Kay Ash notes, "Big success is nothing but a lot of little successes sitting in a row."

Concentrate on each small achievement and you'll undoubtedly have a very successful life.

You must first visualize yourself as a success in order to be successful.

    —**Rosa Diaz,** business executive

[Success] is the ability to see a right idea in spite of the fact that others do not, and to cling to it in the face of discouragement and self-mistrust.

    —**Bette Nesmith Graham,** inventor, business executive

Achievement is not about what you've *done*, but what you've gained from your experience.

    —**Lynn Hill,** rock climber

I personally measure success in terms of the contributions an individual makes to her or his fellow human beings.

    —**Margaret Mead,** anthropologist, 1901–1977

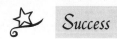

Success is creating something original and lasting—whether it is a company, a work of art, an idea or analysis that influences others, or a happy and productive family.
　　—Linda Chavez, writer, speaker, government official

Ultimately, success is not measured by first-place prizes. It's measured by the road you have traveled: how you have dealt with the challenges and the stumbling blocks you've encountered along the way.
　　—Nicole Haislett, swimmer

Success means pursuing a career that inspires you—brings passion to your life and totally absorbs your energy.
　　—Marin Alsop, conductor

Ninety-eight percent of success is in the head and the heart.
　　—Cathy Ferguson, swimmer

Know the difference between success and fame. Success is Mother Teresa. Fame is Madonna.
—**Erma Bombeck,** writer, humorist, 1927–1996

It's how you deal with failure, not how you deal with success, that determines who, in the end, really makes it.
—**Jane Pratt,** magazine editor

Success doesn't come to you. You go to it.
—**Marva Collins,** teacher

Happiness

Some people think of happiness as a goal they must reach ("I'll be happy once I graduate"). Others think happiness is what they ought to feel on their way to the goal. Still others see it as an attitude ("Don't worry, be happy!"). But regardless of the various perspectives, happiness comes down to one thing: feeling good.

We all have favorite activities that brighten our lives. What floats your boat? Maybe it's talking with friends on the phone, working out, or watching a movie. When you have several that you can alternate, you've got the ingredients for true contentment.

Happiness is not a goal, it's a by-product.
>—**Eleanor Roosevelt,** First Lady, humanitarian, 1884–1962

Happiness must be cultivated. It is like character. It is not a thing to be safely let alone for a moment, or it will run to weeds.
>—**Elizabeth Stuart Phelps,** writer, 1815–1852

Happiness is a choice. You grieve, you stomp your feet, you pick yourself up and choose to be happy.
>—**Lucy Lawless,** actor

[Happiness] is not obtained through self-gratification but through fidelity to a worthy purpose.
>—**Helen Keller,** writer, lecturer, 1880–1968

Happiness is an attitude. We either make ourselves miserable, or happy and strong. The amount of work is the same.
>—**Francesca Reigler,** artist

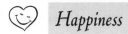

Happiness is a gift. But it cannot be given to you by other people, you give it to yourself.
> —**Jacqueline Kehoe,** age fourteen

One is happy as a result of one's own efforts, once one knows the necessary ingredients of happiness—simple tastes, a certain degree of courage, self-denial to a point, love of work, and above all, a clear conscience.
> —**George Sand (Amandine-Aurore-Lucie Dupin, baronne Dudevant),** writer, 1804–1876

Happiness is not a station you arrive at, but a manner of traveling.
> —**Margaret Lee Runbeck,** writer, 1910–1956

Exude happiness and you will feel it back a thousand times.
> —**Joan Lunden,** TV show host

I do not like the idea of happiness—it is too momentary—I would say that I was always busy and interested in something—interest has more meaning than happiness.
  —**Georgia O'Keeffe,** artist, 1887–1986

The world is extremely interesting to a joyful soul.
  —**Alexandra Stoddard,** author

 Freedom

Think how you would feel if you couldn't make your own decisions and live as you choose.

Did you know millions of women and girls in the world don't have this basic right? In some countries, they are second-class citizens who must obey their husbands and brothers without question.

You are growing up free now because our grandmothers and their ancestors demanded this right and stopped at nothing to get it. Remember—it was only in 1920 that women won the right to vote in the United States! That's why it's important to celebrate your freedom and fight to help others gain their own.

There is a word sweeter than Mother, Home or Heaven—
that word is Liberty.
> —**Gravestone of Matilda Joslyn Gage,** writer, women's
> rights activist, 1826–1898

What can be heavier in wealth than freedom?
> —**Sylvia Ashton-Warner,** educator, writer, 1909–1984

Freedom
Is dearer than bread or joy.
> —**Jessie E. Sampter,** poet, politician, 1883–1938

Freedom unexercised may become freedom forfeited.
> —**Margaret Chase Smith,** congresswoman, 1897–1995

Women must enjoy the right to participate fully in the
social and political lives of their countries if we want freedom
and democracy to thrive and endure.
> —**Hillary Rodham Clinton,** First Lady

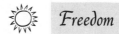

True emancipation begins neither at the polls nor in the courts. It begins in woman's soul.
   —**Emma Goldman,** anarchist, 1869–1940

I always preferred having wings to having things.
   —**Pat Schroeder,** former U.S. congresswoman

Free choice is the greatest gift God gives to his children.
   —**Elizabeth Kübler-Ross,** psychiatrist

The point is less what we choose than that we have the power to make a choice.
   —**Gloria Steinem,** women's rights activist, writer

Chapter 42

 Sisterhood

As writer Robin Morgan once proclaimed, "Sisterhood is powerful." Today, women and girls are reaching out to one another and banding together in all kinds of ways. There's Lilith Fair, the concert tour featuring female performers, the Ms. Foundation's "Take Our Daughters to Work Day," and even "Women's History Month" (March).

But you don't have to wait for formal opportunities such as these; you can celebrate sisterhood in your everyday life. Support and encourage the girls and women in your life: your sisters, your girlfriends, grandmother, aunt, neighbor, the waitress at the local burger joint, the candidate for mayor—whomever, whenever—in whatever they're trying to accomplish!

Not only can women get along beautifully, there is a real camaraderie there.

—**Sheryl Crow,** singer-songwriter

Someone once called me the ultimate cheerleader and I am because I believe that if we do things together, there's hope.

—**Wilma Mankiller,** former principal chief of Cherokee Nation

We are not alone. Beside every successful woman is a group of supportive friends and respectful colleagues. Our belief in one another is what unites us and encourages us to be our best.

—**Sarah McLachlan,** singer-songwriter

All of us working together, in harmony with the Supreme Powers of Nature, is the essence of world power, peace, and tranquillity.

—**Faith Ringgold,** artist

We must be true to each other.
> —**Lucy Stone,** abolitionist, suffragist, 1818–1893

The one hand trying to wash itself is a pitiful spectacle, but when one hand washes the other, power is increased, and it becomes a force to be reckoned with.
> —**Maya Angelou,** poet, writer

We must trust each other.... We must protect our own basic rights by protecting the rights of others.
> —**Faye Wattleton,** health organization leader

There is a mountaintop with enough room for all of us. None of us will get there and stay unless all of us get there and stay there.
> —**Marianne Williamson,** writer, speaker

Women can make sure that as long as we are leaning on each other, we are also protecting and celebrating one another.
   —**Sonja D. Curry-Johnson,** writer

Together we have a voice!
   —**Folashade Oni,** age sixteen

Chapter 43

Giving Back

Pick up today's newspaper and read the headlines. They might be about global warming and pollution, war, AIDS, or homelessness. Most of us feel hopeless when we read these kinds of stories. We wonder what we, as individuals, could ever do to solve problems this big.

You might be surprised.

When she was eleven, Melissa Poe started a club called Kids for a Clean Environment, which now has more than two thousand chapters around the world. Among their projects, the group's members have planted more than four thousand trees.

It's your turn. Pick a cause that fires you up and become the "resident expert."

Who knows? The next time you pick up the newspaper, some of the headlines could be good news.

Have the courage and the daring to think that you can make a difference. That's what being young is all about.
    —**Ruby Dee,** actor, poet

Making a change in one person's life is what keeps me going.
    —**Amber Coffman,** sixteen, founder of nonprofit for the homeless

Let how you live your life stand for something, no matter how small and incidental it may seem.
    —**Jodie Foster,** actor, director, movie producer

In every community there is work to be done.... In every heart there is the power to do it.
    —**Marianne Williamson,** writer, speaker

If you have a bit of knowledge, a piece of information, or some love to give, you ought to give it up.
    —**Lauryn Hill,** singer

As stewards of this planet, we need to make sure that we don't damage it. And if we can, we must leave it better than when we came.

  —**Sandra Day O'Connor,** U.S. Supreme Court justice

How lovely to think that no one need wait a moment, we can start now, start slowly changing the world!

  —**Anne Frank,** diarist, 1929–1945

I think I make a smidgen of a difference every day. That's my ultimate goal—on a daily basis to make a difference in somebody's life, even if it's just my own.

  —**Luana Lacy,** probation officer

If one is going to change things, one has to make a fuss and catch the eye of the world.

  —**Elizabeth Janeway,** writer

So often we think we have got to make a difference and be a big dog. Let us just try to be little fleas biting. Enough fleas biting strategically can make a very big dog very uncomfortable.
—**Marian Wright Edelman,** children's advocate, writer

Our work as citizens is a lot like housework: It never ends. We can either wring our hands in despair or use them to roll up our shirtsleeves and try to find new ways to make a difference.
—**Pat Schroeder,** former U.S. congresswoman

We are rich only through what we give.
—**Anne-Sophie Swetchine,** writer, 1782–1857

You have to take your little piece of the world that needs to be worked on and do the best you can, whatever it is....You have to start small, at the beginning, and that's yourself.
—**Janet McCloud,** Native American activist

Never doubt that a small group of thoughtful, committed citizens can change the world. Indeed, it is the only thing that ever has.

—**Margaret Mead,** anthropologist, 1901–1977

Fun

Now that you've absorbed so much wisdom about life, it's time for the final piece of advice: HAVE FUN!

Dance to a great song, read a good novel, plant a vegetable garden, hang out at a cafe and people-watch, ride a roller-coaster, play volleyball, surf girls' Internet sites, build a fort in your bedroom . . . or whatever your heart desires.

LET THE FUN BEGIN!

Having fun is simply holding on to the joy of each day. It's looking up at the sky and taking a deep breath just because it feels good.... The joy of being a kid, and a girl-kid at that, is one that you can hold on to forever.

—**Judith Harlan,** writer

If someone said, "Write a sentence about your life," I'd write, "I want to go outside and play."

—**Jenna Elfman,** actor

To live exhilaratingly in and for the moment is deadly serious work, fun of the most exhausting sort.

—**Barbara Grizzuti Harrison,** writer, publicist

Be as outrageous as you want to be.

—**Peggy Klaus,** business executive, speaker

Whether you are talking about education, career, or service, you are talking about life. And life must really have joy. It's supposed to be fun.

— **Barbara Bush,** former First Lady

If animals play, this is because play is useful in the struggle for survival: because play practises and so perfects the skills needed in adult life.

— **Susanna Millar,** psychologist, writer

[Life] is big, broad, splendid in opportunity. It is to be used, not cherished. It is to be spent, not saved.

— **Alice Foote MacDougall,** business executive, 1867–1945

Life is a verb, not a noun.

— **Charlotte Perkins Gilman,** writer, lecturer, 1860–1935

I know that I am essentially a sort of fun-loving person who really just wants to sit around and eat pies.
  —**Nora Ephron,** writer

Endings

Here you are at the end of the book.

That's good. Why? Because any time something ends, something else *begins*. In this case, the book is ending, but your exciting life is just beginning!

Start this first day of the rest of your life by imagining yourself wearing a "necklace" of the pearls of wisdom you've collected from this book. You've got a wealth of info that you can use to make it in the world and to carve out your rightful place in it.

Call upon this wisdom whenever you need it, and use it to help make your dreams come true.

The adventure is over. Everything gets over.... Except the part you carry with you.

—**E. L. Konigsburg,** writer

Index